W9-DIJ-180

ULTIMATE MILITARY MACHINES

HELICOPTERS

Tim Cooke

A⁺

Smart Apple Media

This edition published in 2013 by
Smart Apple Media, an imprint of Black Rabbit Books
PO Box 3263, Mankato, MN 56002

www.blackrabbitbooks.com

© 2012 Brown Bear Books Limited

Brown Bear Books Ltd.
Editorial Director: Lindsey Lowe
Managing Editor: Tim Cooke
Children's Publisher: Anne O'Daly
Picture Manager: Sophie Mortimer
Creative Director: Jeni Child

Library of Congress Cataloging-in-Publication Data
Helicopters / edited by Tim Cooke.
       p. cm. -- (Ultimate military machines)
 Includes index.
 Summary: "Describes helicopters as used in the military, including specs, weapons, and crews. Includes the types of
missions they are used in and diagrams of the interior of the vehicle. Features a gallery of helicopters from around the
world."—Provided by publisher.
 Audience: Grades 4-6.
 ISBN 978-1-59920-821-3 (library binding)
 1. Military helicopters--Juvenile literature. I. Cooke, Tim, 1961-
 UG1230.H45 2013
 623.74'6047--dc23
                                       2012006749

Printed in the United States of America at Corporate Graphics, North Mankato, Minnesota

Picture Credits

Front Cover: U.S. Department of Defense

EADS: 28; Getty Images: Scott Peterson 24, 25tl; National Defence, Canada: 16; Robert Hunt Library: 05tl, 08cl, 19tr, 21tr,
21b; U.S. Airforce: 04, 09t, 11bl, 12, 19b, 22br, 23cr; U.S. Army: 09b, 11c, 13t; U.S. Coast Guard: 10br; U.S. Department
of Defense: 05cl, 05br, 06bl, 07tl, 07b, 08br, 13br, 14tl, 14br, 15cr, 17t, 17br, 20cr, 20b, 25br, 26br, 29bl; U.S. Marine
Corps:18, 23cl, 26tl, 27, 29tr; U.S. Navy: 10cl, 10cr, 15b, 22cl.
All Artworks: Windmill Books.

Key: t = top, c = center, b = bottom, l = left, r = right.

PO1438
2-2012

9 8 7 6 5 4 3 2 1

CONTENTS

INTRODUCTION

Skimming the trees to land an assault force in enemy territory or to rescue the wounded, the helicopter is an essential military workhorse. The whir of rotor blades is the sound track of modern warfare. But only 50 years ago, the helicopter was unknown on the battlefeld.

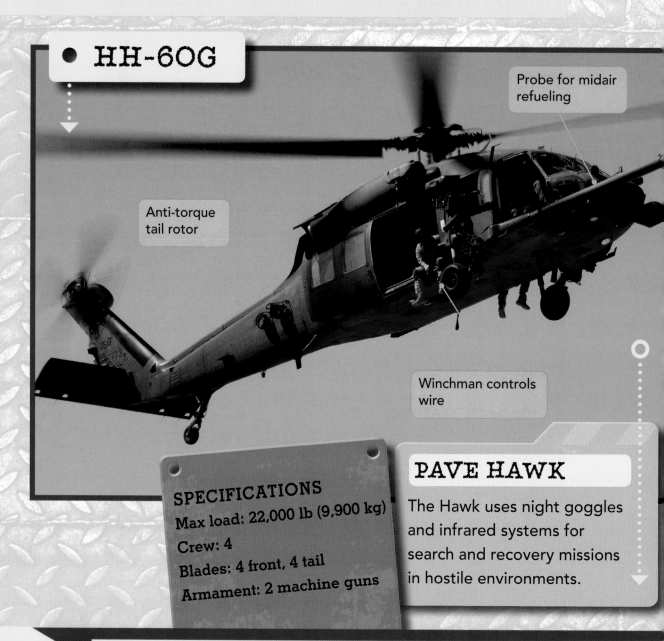

HH-60G

Probe for midair refueling

Anti-torque tail rotor

Winchman controls wire

SPECIFICATIONS
Max load: 22,000 lb (9,900 kg)

Crew: 4

Blades: 4 front, 4 tail

Armament: 2 machine guns

PAVE HAWK

The Hawk uses night goggles and infrared systems for search and recovery missions in hostile environments.

ANTI-TORQUE: Prevents the rotors spinning the aircraft around

AN AGE-OLD DREAM

For centuries, inventors imagined using spinning blades to power an aircraft. Italian artist Leonardo da Vinci invented a version of a helicopter over 500 years ago. But it was not until the 1920s that the first rotorcraft lifted into the air.

◀ Da Vinci invented his corkscrew craft in the 1490s, but it was never built.

● SIKORSKY R4

WORLD WAR II

The Sikorsky R4 was the only mass-produced military chopper of World War II (1939–1945).

THE KOREAN WAR

The Korean War (1950–1953) saw the first real use of helicopters in a war zone. They were mainly used to transport supplies and wounded soldiers.

A Sikorsky hovers above the ▲ ground in Korea while Marines load weapons into its cargo net.

ROTORCRAFT: A flying machine powered by a spinning blade or rotor.

WHAT IS A HELICOPTER?

A helicopter is any aircraft that takes off and lands vertically by using rotor blades to lift the craft into the air. Because helicopters can get to remote areas without landing strips, they are far more flexible than ordinary airplanes.

CONVOY

DEFENSE

Helicopters are great combat machines. They fly low and hug the contours of the land. Their quiet engines and electronic defenses help protect them.

▲ A line of Pave Hawks flies low on a mission. Helicopters often fly in groups so that they can protect one another from attack.

CONTOURS: The way a landscape rises and falls.

UH-1 HUEY

◀ Troops rappel down ropes while a UH-1 Huey hovers.

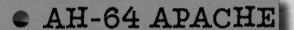

DELIVERY

One of the helicopter's key roles is to get troops or supplies into or out of the battle zone. Helicopters mean that a force does not have to keep land routes open.

AH-64 APACHE

Four blades

30mm M230 chain gun

STRIKE WEAPON

Some helicopters carry machine guns and bombs. The 101st Airborne Division used Apaches and Black Hawks to attack the Iraqi capital, Baghdad, in January 1991.

▲ The AH-64 Apache attack helicopter is used to lead combat missions.

RAPPEL: Descend quickly climbing down a rope.

HELICOPTER MISSIONS

Helicopters have many different roles. They carry personnel and supplies; they gather information; they destroy enemy tanks or submarines. But it is their ability to go anywhere that makes them so valuable to the military.

● BELL UH-1 HUEY

Twin blades and a single engine

◀ The Huey is the world's most popular helicopter. It first flew in 1956 and played a key role during the Vietnam conflict (1964–1973).

RESCUE

An H-5 picks up wounded Marines in Vietnam. Helicopters are vital to get wounded soldiers to field hospitals.

FIELD HOSPITAL: A temporary hospital set up behind the front line.

AH-1 COBRA

STRIKE FORCE

Armed with tube-launched missiles, Cobras target enemy tanks and armored fighting vehicles. They destroyed more than 200 Iraqi tanks during Operation Desert Storm.

SPECIFICATIONS

Max load: 10,000 lb (4,500 kg)
Crew: 2
Blades: 2 main, 2 tail
Main armament: 4 or 8 guided missiles

SPECIAL OPS

Helicopters are ideal for covert operations. They are the best way to get special forces behind enemy lines without being discovered. Helicopters can also rescue personnel if a mission goes wrong.

COVERT: A military operation carried out in secret.

AT SEA

Helicopters are especially useful at sea. Needing little space, they can take off from and land on ships. They can hover for long periods, so they are ideal for search and rescue missions.

MAKING WAVES

An antisubmarine warfare (ASW) MH-60R Seahawk lowers a sonar buoy. If the buoy finds an enemy submarine, the chopper attacks with mines and depth charges.

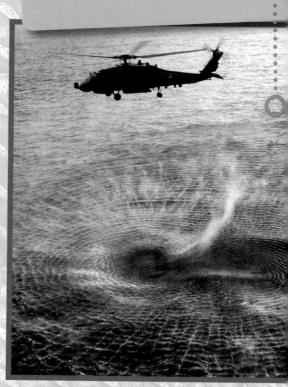

▲ An SH3 Sea King stands by on an aircraft carrier and is ready to rescue downed pilots.

COAST GUARD

Helicopters such as this HH-60 Jayhawk are vital to the US Coast Guard. They are used for rescue and to patrol the country's long coastlines.

SONAR BUOY: A receiver that detects underwater sounds.

HEAVY DUTY

Transporter helicopters use twin rotors to lift heavy loads into a war zone. They can carry combat squads, artillery, or even tanks. Whatever the load, the helicopter can take it up to the front line.

HEAVYWEIGHT

The Chinook has been vital to military campaigns in Vietnam, Iraq, and Afghanistan. Its ability to carry heavy loads has been crucial.

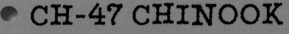

CH-47 CHINOOK

Cargo hooks can carry bulldozers

Wide loading ramp at rear

SUPPLY DROP

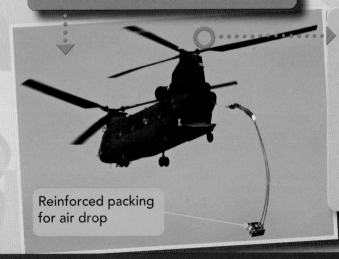

TRANSPORTER

The Chinook uses its rear ramp to drop cargo or personnel by parachute. Its cargo hold can carry 19,500 lb (8,845 kg) of gear or up to 33 troops in full combat gear.

Reinforced packing for air drop

AIR DROP: Delivery of supplies from an aircraft, often by parachute.

HELICOPTER FIREPOWER

Helicopters carry different levels of weaponry. Some are not armed, while others carry machine guns. A navy helicopter carries antisubmarine and antiship missiles. An army gunship combines machine guns with missiles and rockets to support ground troops.

MI-24 HIND

The Russian Mi-24 Hind is a fast gunship and attack helicopter. It carries a combination of machine guns, missiles, rockets, and grenades.

"[That] helicopters are eagerly sought in large numbers by air forces ... all over the world serves to underscore their value."
BILL GUNSTON, RAF PILOT & INSTRUCTOR

● GUNSHIP

"Double bubble" cockpit for pilot and gunner

Stub wings carry weapons

GUNSHIP: A helicopter that carries a powerful range of weapons.

EUROCOPTER TIGER

MULTITASKERS

European Tigers are employed as strike aircraft but are also used for reconnaissance. Unlike other helicopters, the pilot sits in the front and the gunner sits in back. Eurocopters served in Afghanistan and Libya in 2011.

▲ The Eurocopter Tiger came into service in 2003. It is made from composite materials that can withstand cannon fire.

HEAVILY ARMED

The AH-1W Super Cobra carries four missiles on each wing. Its weapon power has made the Cobra a popular choice for the US military since the Vietnam War.

Four missiles carried beneath stub wing

Rocket launcher

▶ Engineers on a US warship inspect the rockets on an AH-1W Super Cobra before a mission.

COMPOSITE: A strong material formed by combining other materials.

ROCKETS

Rockets are powered by their own propellant and are used against aerial and ground targets. In the 1940s, the US Navy developed FFARS, folding-fin aerial rockets, to launch from aircraft.

HYDRA FFARS

SON OF MOUSE

The Hydra 70 is a modern form of the original FFAR, Mighty Mouse. The folding fins make the rockets easier to carry. The rockets can destroy a small tank or attack personnel.

Wire-guided missiles are steered by thin wires attached to the helicopter. The wire uncoils as the missile flies toward its target.

SS-11

▶ The SS-11 wire-guided antitank missile was used until the late 1980s.

TEST AIRCRAFT

PROPELLANT: Fuel that powers an engine to create motion.

HAWK FAMILY

The Sikorsky Black Hawk UH-60 is highly flexible. Because it is easy to maneuver, it can be used in a range of combat roles. As well as carrying different weapons, it is used as a troop and cargo transporter.

▶ The Black Hawk's storage pods carry extra fuel and weapons for long-range operations.

BLACK HAWK

MH-60 SEAHAWK

Based on the UH-60 Black Hawk, the Seahawk is used on aircraft carriers for search and rescue at sea and in combat. With its hinged tail, it does not take up too much room on board.

SEAHAWK

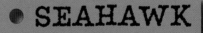

STORAGE POD: A hard-shelled case carried on a heilcopter's wing.

HELICOPTER CREW

A helicopter carries various crew members. The pilot flies the aircraft, which takes a high level of coordination. Some helicopters carry gunners or weapons specialists. A winchman can be lowered to the ground on a cable.

SKILLED PILOTS

Helicopters are difficult to fly. A pilot has to make constant adjustments to keep the aircraft steady in bad weather or when under attack. The job needs high powers of concentration.

"The ability of the helicopter to hover and move in any direction ... gives a thrill."
JOHN FAY, WESTLAND TEST PILOT

COORDINATION: The ability to make different movements at once.

● DOWNWARD

▲ A UH-60 Black Hawk lowers a winchman. At times like this, a helicopter is an easy target. The crew must get the job done fast.

WINCHMAN

Winchmen make rescues when a helicopter cannot land, such as over water or in mountains. The winch can raise an injured patient in a special stretcher.

CONTROL

Helicopter missions are run by air traffic controllers. They use radar to help avoid midair collisions or to direct landings and takeoffs onboard aircraft carriers.

WINCH: A mechanical drum that winds and unwinds a rope or cable.

A CHANGING ROLE

Helicopter crews constantly have to adapt to changes in their enemy's tactics. But they use the helicopter's strengths to their best advantage.

CH-53D

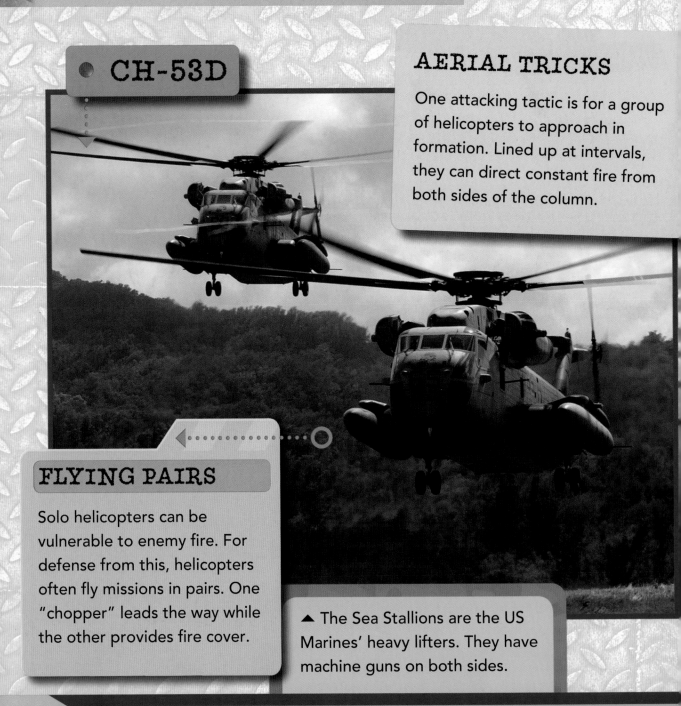

AERIAL TRICKS

One attacking tactic is for a group of helicopters to approach in formation. Lined up at intervals, they can direct constant fire from both sides of the column.

FLYING PAIRS

Solo helicopters can be vulnerable to enemy fire. For defense from this, helicopters often fly missions in pairs. One "chopper" leads the way while the other provides fire cover.

▲ The Sea Stallions are the US Marines' heavy lifters. They have machine guns on both sides.

FIRE COVER: Firing at the enemy to prevent it firing at another target.

UP AND DOWN

A helicopter is far more maneuverable than a fixed-wing airplane. It has VTOL (vertical takeoff and landing), so it can get to remote sites. It can hover in one place. It can even go backward. Pilots learn to maneuver quickly, tipping the helicopter this way and that.

▲ A French Super Puma banks steeply to avoid enemy fire.

APACHE AH64

SPECIFICATIONS
Max load: 23,000 lb (10,433 kg)
Crew: 2
Blades: 4 front, 4 tail
Armament: Hellfire missile

PEEK-A-BOO

The Apache AH-64 catches the enemy unawares. Flying low, it stays hidden by hills, forests, or buildings before it leaves cover to fire its antitank missiles. It is ideal for armed reconnaissance.

RECONNAISSANCE: Learning information about enemy activity.

HELICOPTER HISTORY

The combat role of helicopters has changed. First used in the Korean War, they mainly evacuated wounded soldiers. Today, they are used in the hunt for terrorists in inaccessible mountain regions.

KOREAN WAR

In the Korean War (1950–1953), combat often took place miles from medical help. Helicopters took the wounded to Mobile Army Surgical Hospitals (MASH). Rapid evacuation saved many lives.

◀ An injured US infantryman is lifted onto a helicopter that will take him to a hospital during the Korean War.

▼ A casevac helicopter carried casualties to a MASH, which had lifesaving equipment and a trained medical team.

CASEVAC: A military term for casualty evacuation.

VIETNAM

The use of helicopters changed dramatically in the Vietnam War (1964–1973). Vietnam's mountainous jungles were better suited to helicopters than airplanes. The US Army used its helicopters to transport goods and troops as well as to carry out attack missions.

▶ A wounded US soldier is carried from the UH-1 Huey that has just evacuated him from the battle zone.

● HUEY HELP

● UH-1

◀ Hueys carried troops on missions in Vietnam. Helicopters were useful where there were no roads.

RESCUE

Helicopter search and rescue missions have saved many civilians as well as soldiers. The US Coast Guard, Air National Guard and local rescue teams are kept busy rescuing people from anywhere they get into trouble.

"If a man is in need of rescue ... a direct lift aircraft could come in and save his life."

IGOR SIKORSKY

PLUCKED FROM THE SEA

A helicopter from the USS *Kearsarge* hoists a seriously ill man from a ship in the Caribbean Sea in 2008. The helicopter answered a distress call from the Norwegian vessel.

HH-60 PAVE HAW

ON THE WAY

A winchman from an Air National Guard HH-60 Pave Hawk climbs down a rope ladder to rescue a swimmer from rough water beneath the Golden Gate Bridge in San Francisco.

EVACUATION: Moving someone from danger to safety.

BOSNIA

Since the end of World War II, the helicopter has been called into service across the globe. Peacekeeping forces now operate worldwide. During the 1990s, US military personnel served in Bosnia in Europe. Since then, they have been engaged in Afghanistan and the Middle East.

SAVING SCOTT

In June 1995, US Air Force pilot Scott O'Grady was shot down over hostile territory in Bosnia. Marine CH-53 helicopters from USS *Kearsarge* were deployed to find him. It took a week to locate and rescue Captain O'Grady.

▲ A Sea Stallion lands on USS *Kearsarge* during Operation Enduring Freedom, the US-led fight against global terrorism.

"When in desperate need of evacuation, the approach of a rescue helicopter breaks down all cultural or language barriers."

MICHAEL HAMPSON, HELICOPTER EXPERT

MODERN WARFARE

US helicopters play a key role in the United Nations (UN) peacekeeping force that operates worldwide. The UN has responded to attacks from terrorists and militia in Africa, Europe, the Middle East, and Asia.

BLACK HAWK DOWN

In 1993, elite US soldiers went to Somalia in Africa to capture the warlord who had taken control of the capital, Mogadishu. Two Black Hawks were shot down. US special forces fought to rescue their trapped colleagues, but there were many casualties.

"We got a Black Hawk going down. We got a Black Hawk going down. We got a Black Hawk crashed in the city."
US RADIO TRAFFIC, MOGADISHU, OCTOBER 3, 1993

MILITIA: An irregular fighting unit formed by armed civilians.

DESTROYED

This is the wreckage of a
Black Hawk on the ground
in Somalia. It was shot down
during the Battle of Mogadishu
on October 3 and 4, 1993.

ENDURING FREEDOM

Since 2001, coalition forces have been in
Afghanistan as part of Operation Enduring
Freedom. Helicopters are used to carry troops
and supplies to forward
bases in hostile areas, such as
Helmand province.

▼ A ground crew unloads
a UH-60 Black Hawk from a
C-17 Globemaster transport
plane in Afghanistan in 2002.

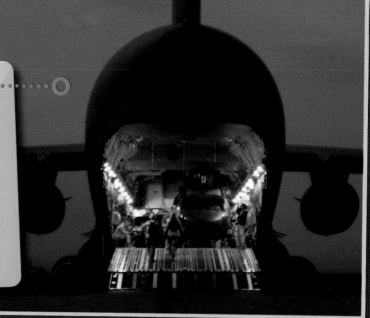

SAFE DELIVERY

Helicopters are vital for moving
troops around Afghanistan. The
Taliban booby-trap the roads
with explosive devices, so air
transportation is much safer than
road transportation.

TALIBAN: An extreme Islamic group that once governed Afghanistan.

GALLERY

Helicopters can be lightning-fast gunships or huge transporters. Their tasks vary from reconaissance and special forces infiltration to medivac and air strikes on enemy targets.

 AH-1W SUPER COBRA

First used by the Americans in Vietnam, the Super Cobra set the standard for other choppers. It has been in use for over 40 years.

SPECIFICATIONS
Max load: 14,750 lb
(6,690 kg)
Crew: 2
Blades: 2 front, 2 tail
Main armament: 20mm cannon

CH-47 CHINOOK

The Chinook dates from 1961. It can carry troops, supplies, and vehicles—even smaller helicopters.

SPECIFICATIONS
Max load: 50,000 lb (22,680 kg)
Crew: 3
Blades: 3 front, 3 tail
Main armament: 3 machine guns

MEDIVAC: Military shorthand for medical evacuation.

The Russian-built Mi-24 Hind is a combat-assault helicopter and a gunship. The Soviet Union used it in its war in Afghanistan in the 1980s.

SPECIFICATIONS

Max load: 26,500 lb (12,000 kg)

Crew: 2–3

Blades: 5 front, 3 tail

Armament: 12.7mm machine gun

COMBAT-ASSAULT: A helicopter that carries troops into action.

GALLERY

The Eurocopter HAP Tiger is one of the world's most advanced attack helicopters. The pilot and gunner wear helmet-mounted sights. The Tiger's armor can withstand cannon fire.

HAP TIGER

SPECIFICATIONS

Max load: 13,000 lb (6,000 kg)

Crew: 2

Blades: 4 main, 3 tail

Main armament: 1x 30mm machine gun

HELMET-MOUNTED SIGHTS: Aim at wherever the wearer is looking.

BELL HUEY

SPECIFICATIONS
Max load: 9,500 lb (4,309 kg)
Crew: 1–4
Blades: 4 main, 2 tail
Main armament: 7.62mm
or 0.5 caliber machine gun

The most widely used utility helicopter in the world, the Bell UH-1 or Huey was a workhorse in Vietnam.

AH-64 APACHE

SPECIFICATIONS
Max load: 23,000 lb
(10,433 kg)
Crew: 2
Blades: 4 main, 4 tail
Main armament: Hellfire
guided missile

The AH-64 Apache is the main US Army attack helicopter. It is designed as a fast-response aircraft. It fights best when it is close to the enemy.

FAST RESPONSE: A helicopter ready for action with little warning.

GLOSSARY

air drop To deliver supplies from an aircraft, often by parachute.

anti-torque Prevents the rotors spinning the aircraft around.

casevac A military term for casualty evacuation.

combat-assault A helicopter that carries troops into action.

composite A strong material formed by combining other materials.

contours The way a landscape rises and falls.

coordination The ability to make different movements at once.

covert A military operation carried out in secret.

deployed Personnel who have been sent out for a particular task.

evacuation Moving someone from danger to safety.

fast response A helicopter ready for action with little warning.

field hospital A temporary hospital set up behind the front line.

fire cover Firing at the enemy to prevent it firing at another target.

gunship A helicopter that carries a powerful range of weapons.

helmet-mounted sights Aims at wherever the wearer is looking.

infantry Troops who are trained to fight on foot.

medivac A military term for medical evacuation.

militia An irregular fighting unit formed by armed civilians.

propellant Fuel that powers an engine to create motion.

rappel Term for quickly climbing down a rope.

reconnaissance Learning information about enemy activity.

rotorcraft A flying machine powered by a spinning blade or rotor.

sonar buoy A floating receiver that detects underwater sounds.

storage pod A hard-shelled case carried on a helicopter's wing.

Taliban An extreme Islamic group that once governed Afghanistan.

winch A mechanical drum that winds and unwinds a rope or cable.

FURTHER READING

BOOKS

Braulick, Carrie A. *U.S. Army Helicopters* (Blazers Military Vehicles). Capstone Press, 2006.

David, Jack. *Apache Helicopters* (Torque: Military Machines). Bellwether Media, 2008.

Green, Michael, and Gladys Green. *Weapons Carrier Helicopters: The UH-60 Black Hawks* (Edge Books War Machines). Capstone Press, 2005.

Hansen, Ole Steen. *The AH-64 Apache Helicopter* (Edge Books Cross-Sections). Capstone Press, 2005.

Sweetman, Bill. *Combat Rescue Helicopters: The MH-53 Pave Lows* (Edge Books War Planes). Capstone Press, 2008.

Von Finn, Denny. *HH-60 Pave Hawk Helicopters* (Epic Books: Military Vehicles). Bellwether Media, 2013.

WEBSITES

military.discovery.com/technology/vehicles/helicopters/helicopters-intro.html
Military Channel videos of the top ten helicopters.

www.military-aircraft.org.uk/helicopters/
Copyright free images of military helicopters for school assignments.

inventors.about.com/od/militaryhistoryinventions/ss/helicopter_.htm
Profiles of military helicopters with links to pages on helicopter history.

www.guncopter.com/
Directory of helicopter gunships with profiles and photographs.

INDEX